Bookkeeping

Step by Step Guide to Bookkeeping Principles & Basic Bookkeeping for Small Business

Mark Smith

hardship or damages that may befall them after undertaking information described herein.

Additionally, the information in the following pages is intended only for informational purposes and should thus be thought of as universal. As befitting its nature, it is presented without assurance regarding its prolonged validity or interim quality. Trademarks that are mentioned are done without written consent and can in no way be considered an endorsement from the trademark holder.

Table of Contents

Introduction **6**

Chapter 1: 7

The Basics of Bookkeeping..7

    The Double Entry Method...8

    Source Documents...9

    End of Period Procedures..9

    Compile the Adjusted Trial Balance 11

    Closing the Books 11

    How to Prepare the Reports... 12

Chapter 2: **14**

Managing the Assets, Liabilities and Owner's Equity **14**

    Assets 14

    Liabilities 17

        Personal Liability...17

    Owner's Equity 18

Chapter 3: Using Ledgers to Keep Track of Your

Business Activity...**19**

    Financial Journals 19

        Cash Receipts Journal (CRJ) 20

        Cash Payments Journal (CPJ) 21

        Sales Journal (SJ)... 21

        Sales Return Journal (SRJ)...22

        Purchases Journal (PJ) 22

        Purchase Returns Journal (PRJ) 22

        General Journal (GJ)..22

    The Ledgers 23

        The General Ledger...23

        Accounts Receivable Ledger and the Accounts Payable

        Ledger 23

Chapter 4: Dealing with Depreciation in Your Business....**25**

    Book Depreciation 28

    Tax Depreciation 28

Chapter 5: How to Adjust Any Entry.................................**31**

    Asset Accounts.. 31

    Adjusting the Entries with Liability Accounts.............................35

Chapter 6: The Different Financial Statements **37**

The Balance Sheet 39

Current Assets 41

Non-Current Assets 42

Liabilities.. 42

Owner's Equity.. 43

The Income Statement.. 43

The Multi-Step Format 45

The Single-Step Format.. 45

Statement of Owner's Equity.................................... 46

Cash Flow Statement 48

Operating Activities 50

Investing Activities 51

Financing Activities 51

Supplemental Information 51

Chapter 7: Understanding How Taxes Work for Your

Small Business **52**

The Legal Entity You Choose Can Affect Your Tax Burden.......... 53

You Can Sometimes Deduct More Than You Think..................... 53

Make the Estimated Payments 55

You Must Pay the Self-Employment Tax 56

The Best Tax Deductions for Your Small Business...................... 56

How to Prepare W2's for Your Employees................................ 59

Chapter 8: The Best Bookkeeping Tips for Your

Business.. **62**

Plan for the Major Expenses.. 62

Track All the Expenses.. 63

Record the Deposits Correctly..................................... 64

Set Money Aside to Help You Pay for Your Taxes 65

Keep a Tab on the Invoices That You Have................................. 66

Conclusion **67**

Introduction

Congratulations on downloading *Bookkeeping* and thank you for doing so.

The following chapters will discuss everything a beginner needs to know in order to get started with their small business bookkeeping. Bookkeeping is important. It gives you an accurate and complete look at the finances of your business. It helps you in making important decisions about it and where it will go in the future. And it can even help you when tax season comes around.

This guidebook will bring up a lot of important topics when it comes to bookkeeping for your small business. We will talk about using ledgers, understanding the taxes with your bookkeeping, how to deal with depreciation, adjusting entries in the ledger, and the different financial statements you need to work with including the cash flow statement, income statement and more.

This is a great resource for those who are ready to start a new business but are also worried about how to keep track of all the financial information for that new business. Take some time to check out this guidebook and see how easy it can be to do your small business books.

There are plenty of books on this subject on the market, thanks again for choosing this one! Every effort was made to ensure it is full of as much useful information as possible, please enjoy!

Chapter 1:

The Basics of Bookkeeping

Before we get into some of the more in-depth stuff that comes with bookkeeping, we need to start you off with some of the basics. If you are running a business and you want to have the ability to read your financial records, and actually be able to understand them, then you need to know the basics. This helps you to know more about the financial aspects of your business rather than relying on someone else to give you this information. When you know the complete picture of your finances, you can make better decisions that will increase the growth of your business. Let's get started with some of the basics of bookkeeping!

The Double Entry Method

When you get started with bookkeeping, you will need to learn a method known as double entry bookkeeping. This means that for each of the entries you put into the ledger, there is going to be one credit and one debit. This results in you getting the two columns to equal each other out. After getting it done and the two columns aren't equal, then you know something isn't matching up the right way. The equation that is important for you to remember with the double entry method is assets = liabilities + equity.

The main point of using the double entry method is that it is simple, and it helps you catch errors early on. With a single-entry method, it would be really hard to tell if a mistake was made. You would get an answer at the end of it and assume it was right. You may have to go over the bookkeeping many times to ensure all the information is inserted properly, and there is still a chance that some errors would slip in.

With the double entry method, you are able to make sure that no mistakes are in the information that you put into the ledger. Any time that you put something into the credit column, then it needs to end up in the debit column. Any time that you put something into the debit column, then the same number needs to end up in the credit column as well.

Then, when you go through the information and do all the addition and subtraction, you should end up with the columns equaling zero. This means that both columns, the credit, and the debit need to come out to be the same thing. If you finish these two columns and they don't total out to zero, then you made a mistake in the ledger somewhere and you need to go back thoroughly and find where it is.

Source Documents

Every transaction that you make through your business needs to have a source document. These documents can be a variety of things including a gas receipt to a contract. This is like the proof that you either paid for something or that you made money from the transaction so it is important to have it available. So, if you spent any money on the business, then you must have some kind of source document present in order to prove the amount that you spent at that particular time.

These documents should have at least a few details in them. It will provide you with enough information so that you can record it in the books. It can include the amount of money that you spent, what you spent it on, who you paid the money to, and what you spent the money on. Some of the bookkeeping software that you work with will allow you to attach the scanned file to the transaction to keep them all together, making it easier to see it any time that you need to bring up the source document.

End of Period Procedures

The end of period procedures doesn't just relate to quarters. Even though you have taken the time to record all of your transactions each month through the year, this doesn't mean that they are all read when you prepare those final financial reports.

To make sure that all the books you do are accurate for preparing these financial reports, you need to consider that there are different procedures that you will need to take care of at the end of the month, at the end of the year, or at the end of the payroll year. Some examples of how you would do this include:

The month end procedures:

- Lock periods.
- Pay all the taxes for payroll.
- Record depreciation.
- Send customer statements.
- Review any reports that you have.
- Reconcile all the bank accounts.
- Run the business or the company data auditor.

Year-end procedures (the ones you prepare for a brand new fiscal year):

- Enter all of the end of year adjustments.
- Provide some information to the accountant who will do the work.
- Do an inventory count.
- Complete the month end tasks that we had above.
- Verify and optimize the company or the business file.
- Start a new fiscal year.
- Back up the business or company file.

End of the payroll year (make sure not to update the tax tables at this time):

- Print out the vendor 1099.
- Print your year-end payroll forms.
- Restore all the backup.
- Run the first payroll.
- Install any product updates that are needed at that time.
- Start your new payroll year.
- Make sure that the company or the business file is backed up.

- Optimize and then verify the business file.
- Run the last payroll.
- Print the payroll reports.

Compile the Adjusted Trial Balance

Making all these adjustments may sound time-consuming, but they are important to your business. You may be curious as to which adjustments need to be made first. To help you with this decision, you will need to gather and then compile a spreadsheet. This allows you to put in the trial balance entries and then make any adjustments that are needed.

When working with an adjustment, remember that these are there to correct any errors that came up in the initial trial balance. This way, you get everything balanced when you are done. This form for the adjustments is known as an internal form but will be used to help compile financial statements. If you are using software like QuickBooks or Xero, it is not likely that you would use the trial balance worksheet. It is still a good source document to utilize though. The reason it isn't really used as much though is because those automated systems will do all the reports for you.

Closing the Books

At the end of the fiscal year, you will need to close out your books for that year before starting with something new. When you do this process, there are four main areas that need to be closed. These areas are going to be temporary accounts and you must zero them out at the end of the year to keep your books organized. You will first start by creating your own income summary account, which is known as the holding area. The other things you will need to do to close out the books include:

- Closing out the revenue accounts: You will need to go through the credit or debit of this account so that it is at a zero balance. Then you can either credit or debit the income summary account so that this balance is added to that new account. Remember, if you debit or credit one of the accounts, then you will need to do the opposite to the new account to make it balanced. So, if you debit your revenue account, then you need to credit the income summary account to balance it out.
- Closing the expense account: You will then need to close out your expense account. This account will need the same steps as before so that it is at zero.
- Balance your income summary: By name, you should have an increase in the income summary for the revenue and then a decrease for the other expenses. Keep in mind that if the expenses end up being more than the revenue you get, you will have a negative number here and will have a loss.
- Closing the income summary: The last step to take in closing your books at the end of the year is to debit or credit the income summary account, along with the retained earnings account. This leaves a zero balance in your income summary account and you can move on to the next step.

How to Prepare the Reports

We will talk about this a bit later, but it is important to prepare the right reports or the right financial statements. There are quite a few different reports that you can create, but the main ones that you should become familiar with include the statement of cash flow, the statement of retained earnings, the income statement, and the balance sheet. These are the reports that tell the most about the finances of your business and will be needed if you ever take your business public and put stocks on the stock market.

Chapter 2:

Managing the Assets, Liabilities and Owner's Equity

Before we go too much into some of the financial reports of your business, it is important to consider three areas that you need to manage well in the area of accounting. Knowing these will make it easier to control your business finances and will ensure that you are going to be able to fill out those financial documents later on. The three main areas of accounting that you should consider include the assets, the liabilities, and the owner's equity.

Assets

The first area we are going to explore is the assets. These would be any cash that the business has on hand, as well as anything that the company could sell relatively quickly and make money on. Some of the assets that your business needs to keep track of include:

- Any property or real estate
- Fixed income
- Equipment
- Brokerage services
- Money market accounts,
- Loans that the company made to others
- Debit or credit cards the business holds

If you run a business, you already know that you need some kind of funding to keep the doors open. Therefore, when you are looking at a financial institute to help you get that funding so you can get started, you must make sure to pick out a good bank, one which is able and is willing to give you the loan and work with you as you grow.

Working with a bank and convincing them to give you the funding that you need is important to the well-being of your business. But it can also be one of the hardest parts. You have to convince them that your business is a good one. You need to convince them that you will be able to pay them back. You need to convince them that they won't waste money by helping you out.

While each bank is going to be a little bit different, some of the things that most banks are going to look for include:

- The number of years you have been in business. The longer you have been running your business, the easier it is to get the money.
- A minimum amount of revenue. This also depends on how much money you are asking the bank for.
- A minimum FICO score. Some banks will require you to submit your personal credit before they give any funding.
- Profitability: Does the loan rely on you being able to earn a certain amount of profit to pay it back or not?
- Bankruptcy: If your business, or you personally, has filed for bankruptcy in the past, you may have to look at the rules of that bank to find out if they will still provide you with the loan.
- Credit card volume: Some loans will take a look at your credit card volume for the business before giving you a

loan. This is because those kinds of loans are going to be paid off with the use of volume.

- Accounts receivable: Some types of loans, usually the alternative ones, will want to take a look at your accounts receivable when making a decision.
- Existing debt: The bank oftentimes look at the debt that your business already has and how well you have been able to manage it so far.

Each type of loan that you go for will require different things before you can be approved. For example, a startup loan doesn't require you to be in business at all before applying while a line of credit would need at least a year in business and a Small Business Administration Loan would require that you be in business for at least two years.

You will need to make sure that you are getting all the paperwork in order before you decide to go talk to the bank. This will ensure that you are ready for them and makes it easier to get the funding that you need. A good credit score, a lower balance on any personal or business accounts, all the financial documents for the business, and information on what the funding will be used for can all be useful to the bank when making a decision.

Also, consider shopping around for a bit. You don't have to just go with one bank when it is time to go with funding. Some banks are friendlier to small businesses and some will offer better deals to people who agree to work with them. Talking to a few different banks and finding out what they can offer to you could help you get more of the funding that you need, and could even save you money in the process.

Liabilities

The next thing we are going to look at is the different liabilities of the company. This would be anything that you still owe on, such as a loan from a bank, the amount that you owe to stockholders at the end of the quarter, or anything else that would take money away from the profits that you earn. Customer deposits and fund securities can be examples of a liability.

As a business, it is best if you are able to keep those liabilities to a minimum, although this can be hard if you are just starting out the business. No matter how good you are in the business world and no matter how well you keep the business in control, you will end up with some kind of liability. However, there are ways on how to ensure your business, as well as its assets, the protection it needs from the liabilities when they arise. Let's take a look at some of the ways that you can protect yourself against these liabilities.

Personal Liability

Even though you started your business and incorporated as a Limited Liability Company, it doesn't mean that you won't have any personal liabilities with the business. This is rarer, but when you are starting up, there may be some things that you can do in order to get funding or to get the business off the ground that could hold you personally liable for the business. Some examples of this include:

- You guarantee the loan for funding for the business.
- The actions that you personally do result in the injury.
- You did something illegal with the business or committed some other crime.

- You do not operate the business in a way that makes it separate from your personal accounts.

To help protect yourself, you may want to consider having some business liability insurance. This is going to be there to protect your small business from property damage or personal injury if there is a lawsuit that should come up. There are a few different types of business liability insurance that you can choose to go with including:

- Professional liability insurance: This is going to protect any business owners who provide service to their customers. It could protect you against omissions, negligence, errors, malpractice, and more. This can help protect you in case there is an accident with another person while you provide them a service so you don't end up losing all your personal assets in the process.
- Product liability insurance: This protects you against any financial loss that could occur because of defective products that cause harm to someone.
- General liability insurance: This is a general policy that will protect you against advertising claims, any claim of negligence, property damages, and injury claims.

Owner's Equity

There isn't really one set way for you to manage the owner's equity. This is going to be based off a few things including the investment you get from stocks, the money you put into the company, and the amount that you take out from the company. To handle these transactions, you will just need to use your regular bank account for business and then make sure it is linked up to your bookkeeping software.

Chapter 3:

Using Ledgers to Keep Track of Your Business Activity

Ledgers and journals are going to be one of the most important parts of bookkeeping. These ledgers will hold onto the information for your bookkeeping and keeping them up to date can ensure that your accounting is done the right way. These ledgers and journals will help you to keep track of any transaction that occurs in your business so you know where they come from and so much more. Let's take a look at how each of these work and why they are so important.

Financial Journals

When it comes to journaling for your business and for bookkeeping, you are going to work with a General Journal. If you aren't familiar with this General Journal, you may look it over and get a bit lost on what the numbers mean and how it will impact your business. The General Journal will hold a lot of information, but there are also six other journals, that can either make up this one or be used on their own depending on your business, which can help you keep track of the various transactions that you complete. Some of the journals you can use, in addition to the General Journal, include:

- Purchase returns journal
- Purchase journal
- Sales returns journal
- Sales journal
- Cash payments journal
- Cash receipts journal

These financial journals hold a lot of information for you. Remember that if you deal with any accounting or bookkeeping software, you will not have to deal with these journals on your own. But it is still important to know what they all are and how they can be of benefit to your business.

Cash Receipts Journal (CRJ)

When you receive any cash in your business, you will need to make sure it is recorded in the Cash Receipts Journal. There are different categories that come with the CRJ. These categories include debtors, income, sundry, bank, ref. details, and date.

Any time that you look at your business CRJ, you will see that there are three major categories that will go on the top. The bank is going to be the total of each line and will show you the cash that was received. Income is going to be taken from any receipts that you have where you brought in money. You will also receive a receipt from your debtors any time you paid them out money. The category "sundry" is basically going to be general or miscellaneous payments that you may have.

Cash Payments Journal (CPJ)

Similar to the CRJ, the cash payments journal is going to show you where the cash has been paid out for a business. This one will also have some of the same categories as the CRJ including sundry, creditors, expenses, ref, details, bank and date for each transaction.

If you decide that you would like to use a cash book rather than the general journal, then the CPJ is going to be a combination of your SPJ and the SRJ. This allows the cash book to show you all of the payments and the receipts at the same time. When you use a petty cash fund in your business, you can keep track of this fund with the help of additional journals, and they will work on the same format as the CPJ and CRJ.

Sales Journal (SJ)

Whether your business is going to offer merchandise, services, or a combination of both, sales are going to be so important. And to help you keep track of these sales, a Sales Journal can be the tool that you want. For this kind of journal, only the income on credit will show up. Once this is paid, and the business receives payment or cash for the service, then it will be recorded in the cash receipts journal. Some of the main categories that are present in the Sales Journal include services rendered, ref., debtor and date.

Sales Return Journal (SRJ)

Everytime your company sells a product or merchandise, you will occasionally deal with a customer returning the item. When one of these returns happens, you will need to record this return in the Sales Returns Journal about where it had been originally sold to. The categories that you will find in the SRL includes the sales returns, ref, debtor, and date.

Purchases Journal (PJ)

When the business has some type of inventory, you will also work with the Purchases Journal. This is the journal that you will use when your business purchases inventory on credit. The PJ is only going to apply to the inventory you have. This means you will not purchase all of your assets here. Only the inventory that you purchase using credit should be put on the Purchases Journal. The categories that come with this journal includes purchases, ref, creditor, and the date.

Purchase Returns Journal (PRJ)

Just like when you use the SRJ, the Purchase Returns Journal is going to record any of the merchandise that the business purchased on credit and is then needed to be able to return to the merchandiser. The categories that you will put on your PRJ include purchases returns, ref, creditor, and date.

General Journal (GJ)

The General Journal is the tool that will hold onto all the transactions that your business makes. It will hold onto the information that is found in the other six journals that we talked about. This is a great way to put all the information about transactions in your business in one place.

The Ledgers

When you work with double-entry accounting and bookkeeping, there are three main categories of ledgers that you should look at. These will include:

- General Ledger
- Accounts Receivable Ledger
- Accounts Payable Ledger

It may seem like you are taking up a lot of time to record all of your entries in these ledgers twice. But you want to organize these transactions in both the journals we talked about before as well as in the ledger accounts to help you keep track of things.

The General Ledger

As soon as you set up the bookkeeping for your business, a Chart of Accounts is created. Each account on this chart will have a reference number assigned to it. This helps you to keep track of the different transactions that happen, regardless of whether they are found in the journal or on the ledger. This general ledger is important to help you keep track of your transactions in one place, and when you combine it together with the journals from above, you will be able to keep track of everything financial about your business.

Accounts Receivable Ledger and the Accounts Payable Ledger

These two ledgers are considered subsidiary ledger accounts. These are the accounts that are, in addition to your General

Ledger, will mainly be used so you can accurately track the receivables and the payables of your business.

You may end up having multiple accounts that belong to vendors who you either owe money to or they owe money to you. Each of these accounts needs to have their own ledgers in order to keep things organized. The Accounts Receivable will have a debit normal balance while the Accounts Payable will have a credit normal balance.

Chapter 4:

Dealing with Depreciation in Your Business

At some point when you start on your business, you will need to purchase equipment to help you get the work done. You will need this equipment to last for a few years. However, over the years of its usage, it is going to end up losing its value.

Let's look at an example of this. You purchase a computer for your business that has Windows 7 on it and all the other programs that you need to get things done. This computer costs you $575. After owning and maintaining this computer, it starts to break and you need to find parts.

Over that time, your depreciation went down from $575 to closer to $50. And, since technology is moving so fast as it advances, you find that you can no longer get the parts that you need. Now your depreciation of $50 is considered a recycling fee.

From this example, you can see that the equipment is going to lose its value and we need to calculate this into your bookkeeping somehow. The depreciation can sometimes be an annual income tax deduction. It will be something that you will list as an expense on the income statement. This is a good deduction that is an advantage to you and you can get this by filing the Form 4562 when you file your tax return.

To claim this depreciation deduction, there are a few guidelines that the property needs to meet ahead of time. Some of these requirements include:

- You must actually own the property. It is impossible to depreciate capital improvements for a property that you lease.
- The property must be something that you use for business or to produce income. If you use it for personal and business use, then you are not allowed to deduce the property based only on the business use of the property.
- The property that you are trying to deduct needs to have a reasonable lifespan that is longer than a year.

Even if the property you want to deduct ends up meeting all of these requirements, it may not qualify for the deduction. Some of the properties that you are not able to deduct include:

- Any property that is placed into service and then disposed of the same year.
- Any equipment that you use to build capital improvements. You are able to add in allowable depreciation on the equipment during the construction based on improvements.
- Certain term interests.

For the most part, most of the property that you get and use for business purposes can be depreciated. You are able to depreciate a lot of your property including equipment, furniture, vehicles, machinery, and buildings. You can't depreciate land though, because it is expected that you will use that land for the whole lifetime of your business and it never depreciates in value to you. The building that is on the land can be depreciated when it is time to do taxes that year.

You must take the time to identify which items you want to depreciate and deduct when you are filing your taxes. You will be able to do this with the Form 4562 to help you get started. This ensures that you are properly depreciating any of the property that you use. Some of the items that are found on this Form 4562 include:

- Depreciable basis of the property
- Whether there are any bonuses that you qualify for in the first year of depreciation
- Whether you elect to expense out any portion of the asset
- Whether the property is listed property
- Class life of the asset
- Depreciation method for your property

The next question is all about how you are supposed to calculate what the depreciation of the property is. There are two main methods that you can use to do this. These include tax depreciation and book depreciation.

Book Depreciation

To start with, you can work with book depreciation. This is used often for bookkeeping and accounting purposes. The goal for using this depreciation type is to match the cost of an asset with the revenue that it earns over the period of its lifetime. The common method that you will use for this method is known as the straight-line method. This is calculated with one of the two formulas that are below:

- Annual depreciation = (Cost − Residual Value) / Useful Life
- Annual depreciation = (Cost − Residual Value) * Rate of depreciation.

There are several categories that you will need to fill in for both of these in order to get the answers that you need. The different parts defined are below:

- Cost: This is the original amount that you paid for the equipment or the property.
- Residual value: This is sometimes called the scrap value. This is the question of what will be the value of the property or equipment at the end of its use.
- Useful life: This is the amount of time that you plan to use and keep the equipment before you get rid of it or upgrade to something else.
- The rate of depreciation: This is the percentage of the useful life-span that is used in an accounting period.

Tax Depreciation

There are a lot of different methods that you can use to calculate the depreciation of the property. This means that you are not stuck working with just one type if you don't like it or it doesn't work for your bookkeeping needs. When you are working on your taxes though, the IRS likes to work with the accelerated depreciation method the best.

This is a method that will return more of your money in the first year or two of the asset's life, rather than expanding it out through the years. There are a few different methods that can be used to help with accelerated depreciation.

The first method is the declining balance depreciation. This is going to use the following formula to come up with the amount of depreciation for your property:

- Declining balance depreciation = Rate * Net book value

You can also choose to work with what is known as the double declining balance method to help you come up with the depreciation. The formula to use for this one is:

- Double declining rate = 2/useful life
- Double declining balance depreciation = net book value * 2 / useful life

When you are working on the depreciation of an item or property, make sure that you keep all of the receipts. There may be a time when you need to prove how much the worth of the item is, where you bought it, and so on. Having this information present and written out in a receipt will make it easier for the auditors (if any show up), your accountant, or your bookkeeper to check to make sure that you are getting the right amount of depreciation and that there are no mistakes at tax time.

The depreciation of your property can help you save money at tax time. You can regain some of the value of that item back throughout the years in your taxes, as long as the property ends up depreciating and you use it for your business use. If you are uncertain about whether or not you are able to depreciate an item from your business or how much you are able to get from depreciation, make sure to talk to your accountant to help you here.

Chapter 5:

How to Adjust Any Entry

As you are working with your small business, you may find that there are times when you need to adjust some of the entries that you put in for bookkeeping. These journal entries will be able to turn your accounting records into accrual-based accounting. These are the entries that you will want to make prior to issuing the financial statements.

In many cases, when you want to adjust an entry, you are doing it because you need to fix some of your expenses. However, you may need to use this for other things as well, including making adjustments for revenue. Basically, there are two scenarios where adjusting entry is needed before the financial statements are issued and these include:

1. When nothing has been put into the accounting records for a certain revenue or expenses. These revenues or expenses did occur and they should be included in the current balance sheet or income statement for that period, so an adjustment is necessary.
2. When there has been an entry into the records, but the amount needs to be divided up because it occurs through more than one accounting period.

Asset Accounts

Any time that you are trying to make some adjustments to the entries that you have, you need to take the time to assure that both the income statement and the balance sheet are done properly so that they check out with each other. While we will talk about both of these financial statements in the next chapter, this basically means that both these statements need to be up to date based on the accrual basis of accounting.

The best way to go through and do this is to examine and then review each of the balances that are on your balance sheet. Let's take a look at the following example and then break it down to get a better idea of what is going on. Remember, this is based on the account balances that were done before any of the adjustments were added. The different areas that we will focus on here will include the following:

- Cash: $1,800
- Accounts Receivable: $4,600
- Allowance for doubtful accounts: $0
- Supplies: $1,100
- Prepared insurance: $1,500
- Accumulated depreciation equipment: $7,500
- Equipment: $25,000

Let's break this down now that we have all the numbers. Looking at the general ledger, the cash account is showing there is a balance of $1,800 in cash. However, before you use this information to create your balance sheet, there are two questions that you need to ask yourself. First, ask whether the $1,800 is the true amount of cash or not? Second, ask if this agrees with what was figured based on your bank reconciliation.

If the cash doesn't match with what you found out when you did the bank reconciliation, then you need to go through and make some adjustments so that the balance sheet has the right information. Some examples of needing to do this would be to check printing charges, banking fees, or service charges. These entries need to be added to the cash account so that it matches up with your bank statements.

Then you need to take a look at the accounts receivable. For this account, you need to take a look at any of the unpaid invoices that you have. These can be found on the subsidiary ledger for accounts receivable. For this, we are going to assume that the $4,600 that we had above is accurate for all the amounts that were not paid as of yet.

The balance sheets will need to report all of the amounts. This should also include the money that has not yet been paid but is still due to the business. This can also go for all the revenue that has been billed at that time as well. After a review, you find out that $3,000 of services has been earned. This was dated as something that occurred on December 31, but it was not billed until January 20. In order to have that information show up on your December financial statements, you would need to go through and make an adjusting entry.

Remember that when you do your entries, they all need to have at least one credit and one debit. The two accounts that you would do in this will be the Service Revenue and the Accounts Receivable. The Accounts Receivable will have the normal debit balance and it will be part of your balance sheet accounts. The Service Revenues have a normal credit balance and also part of the income statement accounts.

When we take a look at the previous balance that we had of $4,600 for this area and then we make the adjusting entry for the $3,000 that needs to be added in, then the new balance on this account is going to be $7,600.

Now we need to work on the allowances for doubtful accounts. If you take a look at your information here, you will notice that this account is not one that is listed on your balance sheet. The reason for this is because it has a balance of $0. It is common for an account that has a balance of $0 to not show up on the balance sheet because it is just going to pretty much take up space.

At one point, there is a possibility that your business has some accounts that have not been collected. The reasons for this can vary. Instead of reducing the Accounts Receivable by issuing a credit on the ledgers, you would add it to this category.

To take a look at this, let's say that your business has $600 that is not going to be collected. This means that you would want to report that $600 in the Allowance for Doubtful Account. There are going to be two accounts that need to be brought in for this transaction. You will have this Allowance for Doubtful Accounts on the balance sheet and this account will have a credit normal balance. Then the other account is going to be the Bad Debts Expense that is on the income statement. This account is going to have a normal debit balance.

As you go through your balance sheet, you need to remember which accounts are going to be affected and which ones will have either a normal debit or credit. From here, you should take some time and practice doing your own bookkeeping. Try to figure out the rest of the adjusting entries for the asset accounts. The numbers that you should use for getting this done and getting some practice include:

- Supplies are $1,100.
- Adjusting entry is $275. The balance for supplies will be $725 and the accounts that you will use to get this done will be Supplies and Supplies Expense.
- Prepaid insurance is $1,500.
- The adjusting entry is going to be $900. The balance for this prepaid insurance will be $600 and the accounts that you will use are Insurance Expense and Prepaid Insurance.
- Equipment is $25,000.
- You do not need to do any adjusting entries here.
- Accumulated depreciation equipment is $7,500.
- Adjusting entry is going to be $15,000. The balance for the accumulated depreciation equipment is going to be $9,000 and the accounts that you will use for this one will be the accumulated depreciation equipment and the depreciation expense equipment.

Adjusting the Entries with Liability Accounts

As you take a review of the accounts that are on your balance sheet, it is not enough to just take a look at the assets and then stop there. The liability accounts should also be reviewed. You want to go through and check out these accounts using the same methods that you used with the assets. The steps to doing this would include the following:

- Notes Payable: $5,000
- There is no adjusting entry that is needed here.
- Interest Payable: $0
- Adjusting entry is $25. The balance for the interest payable is going to be $25 and the accounts that are

involved with this are the Interest Expense and the Interest Payable.

- Accounts Payable: $2,500
- Adjusting entry is $1,000. The balance for the Accounts Payable will be $3,500 and the accounts involved are Accounts Payable and Repairs and Maintenance Expense.
- Wages Payable is $1,200.
- Adjusting entry is $300. The balance of wages payable is going to be $1,500 and the accounts that you will use with this one are the Wages Payable and the Wages Expense.
- Unearned Revenues will be $1,300.
- Adjusting entry is $800. The balance for your Unearned Revenues will be $500 and the accounts involved will include Unearned Revenues and Service Revenues.

When you do this, remember that the normal balance for each of the account is going to be affected. As you go through and adjust the entries, and when you do not know the normal balance for both transactions, you should try to find the one that you do know. There is going to always be a credit and debit for each transaction made. If it has a credit normal balance and then the adjustment ends up increasing the account, then you need to also go through and debit the other account.

Chapter 6:

The Different Financial Statements

As we have mentioned a few times in this guidebook, there are some financial documents that are important to your business. These documents are going to help you keep your finances in line, help you know whether you are making accurate entries into the ledger, and can even assist you when you need to bring in investors or lenders to grow your business.

As an owner of a small business, you need to have a good understanding of some of these basic statements so you can really get a good look at where the business stands financially. This is where it is extremely important for you to always communicate with the bookkeeping.

There are actually quite a few different financial statements that you could look at. The one that you want to work with will depend on what you are interested in finding out. But the most common ones, and the ones that are often seen as the most important include:

- The cash flow statement
- The owner's equity statement
- The income statement
- The balance sheet

These are considered the big 4 because they are going to give you a good picture of where your business is standing financially. They are also the statements that you need to show your investors to make decisions about whether they will work with you or not. Let's take a look at each one and see how they work and why they are so important for your business.

You must make sure that you fill out these financial statements on a regular basis. Most companies will do one each quarter of their business, and then they do this at the end of the year. There are several benefits to doing this. First, it is required for all publicly traded companies through the SEC. You need to submit these four documents to the SEC at these times to remain on the stock exchange.

You will find that a lot of your investors and lenders will take a look at these financial statements. They are able to get a good view of your financial state and can make smart decisions about whether they want to invest in you or give you a loan. Without this information, the investors and the lenders won't even consider you. So, even if the SEC didn't require that you submit this information to them, it can still be useful if you need a business loan to fund something, like new equipment or an expansion, or to help convince investors that your business is a good option.

Another benefit of using these financial statements is that they give you a good view of your financial statement in the business. You will be able to fill them out pretty easily if you have been keeping good records through the other tips that we talked about. You can then compare this information with the financial statements that you completed in previous quarters and years to let you know the trends of your financial state and make good decisions to prepare you for the future.

The Balance Sheet

The first financial document we will look at is the balance sheet. This one is going to use the formula assets = liabilities + equity. Within this particular statement, you will see that these three areas are divided up to show which of your business accounts are listed under the owner's equity, liabilities, and assets.

The owner's equity will represent the earnings that are retained for your business. You will see that all of the accounts that are on this balance sheet do not have to keep a $0 balance. Generally, the accounts with $0 balance are ones that are not on the balance sheet.

You can pick from two types of formats for your balance sheet. You can pick from either the horizontal or the vertical formats. Most businesses prefer to work with the vertical format. But if you want to work more with the accounting equation from before, you will want to work with the horizontal format.

Based on the assets that your business has, the business is going to be balanced in all the obligations of a business financially. This will include investments and any retained earnings. Think about it this way. Assets are the means a business uses to operate. Owner's equity and liabilities are the two main ways that you can support these assets.

The balance sheet is going to be the financial statement that will report all of the assets and liabilities of the company as well as the shareholders' equity, basing this from a specific point in time. It is a going to provide you with a basis for computing rates of return and then evaluating the capital structure of the business.

The neat thing about the balance sheet is that it is really good for providing a snapshot of the company, what that company owes and owns, and also some information about the amount that has been invested by shareholders. It can go in depth or just give an overview of the finances of the business.

Many investors and lenders will take a look at the balance sheet. They do need to look at some of the other financial statements to get the best view of how the company is doing financially. But the balance sheet is a good place for the lenders and the investors to look to in order to see a summary or a snapshot of the company before going further.

Interpreting the balance sheet is not meant to be difficult. This statement is a snapshot that represents the state of the company financially in just one moment of time. By itself, it is not going to show you the trends of the company that have played out over time. Because of this reason, when you are attempting to interpret the balance sheet, you need to compare it with some previous balance sheets. So if you are looking at the balance sheet for the fourth quarter of the company, you should compare to the balance sheets for the third, second, and first quarters as well so you can see the numbers and the trends over the past year.

In addition, it is a good idea to take those balance sheets and then compare them to other businesses that are considered to work in the same industry. This gives you a good idea of whether the company is doing well compared to the trends in the industry or not. Don't compare the balance sheet of a company to those in different industries because each industry will have their own approaches to financing and this can get confusing.

Now that you know a bit more about the balance sheet, it is important to know what accounts need to be listed in each section. These are the owner's equity, liability, and assets. Let's divide each part up to see what will be inside each one on the balance sheet.

Current Assets

The items that you put inside the current assets are the ones that will have a lifespan of a year or less. The business then plans to convert those assets into cash. Some of the items that you can put into the current assets part of the balance statement include:

- Short-term obligations that you owe to the clients
- Accounts receivable
- U.S. Treasuries
- Cash
- Cash and cash equivalents
- Raw materials
- Inventory

Non-Current Assets

These assets are the ones that can't be turned into cash as easily. These are the ones that are expected to be turned into cash within a year, or they could have a longer life span of more than a year. These are the ones that will usually have depreciation associated with them as well. Some examples of these types of assets include:

- Copyright
- Patents
- Goodwill
- Intangible assets
- Land
- Buildings
- Computers
- Machinery
- Tangible assets

Liabilities

When you are looking at your liabilities, you are going to consider this as the obligations that the business owes to others. Just like assets, these can include both long-term and current liabilities. Some of the liabilities that will be found in this column of the balance statement include:

- Non-debts that are more than one year old
- Debts that are more than one year
- Long-term liabilities
- Accounts payable
- Paid within a year
- Current liabilities

Owner's Equity

This is the money that the owner has invested inside of their business. The retained earnings that are shown on your income statement will be transferred into the owner's equity at the end of your fiscal year. The owner's equity is going to show the net worth of the business. You will have a capital account or a drawing account. The capital account is going to be any money invested or earned by the business. The drawing account is going to be the money that is withdrawn from the business.

The Income Statement

When you first take a look at the business statement, there is a lot of information and it can seem scary. However, once you know what is inside of it, you will find that this statement can be really useful. The income statement is going to take a closer look at all the sales and all the expenses of that business. The business can usually choose to do this quarterly and annually through their fiscal year to keep track of things.

An income statement is another financial statement that is going to be responsible for reporting a company's financial performance over a specific period of accounting. The financial performance of a company will be assessed by providing a summary to lenders and investors about how the business will incur all its revenues and expenses through both its non-operating and operating activities.

The income statement is often going to be known as the profit and loss statement, and it is one of the three financial statements that need to be present in the annual report of the company as well as the 10-K. All public companies will need to submit these documents legally to the SEC and the investor public. The other two sheets that are submitted at the same time will be the cash flows statement and the balance sheet.

These three are important because they can provide the investors and the lenders with a lot of information about the state of finances of a business, but the income statement is unique because it is the only one that will summarize the sales and the net income of the company.

Unlike what you would do with the company balance sheet, the income statement is going to provide the performance information about a certain time. While the balance sheet will just say how the business is at the exact time the business owner filled out the sheet, the income statement is going to provide information over a year, a quarter, or a year based on the way that the company records this information. The income statement is going to start off with the sales of the company and then will work its way down to the net income and then the earnings per share.

There are two main parts that need to be present on the income statement, no matter what type of company you are running. These two parts are the non-operating and the operating.

With the operating portion of this financial statement, you will disclose all the information about any revenues and expenses that the company incurred directly from regular business operations. For example, if you are a business that sells sports equipment, you would make your money by selling these pieces of equipment. This information would be recorded in the operating section of this statement.

The income statement also needs to include the non-operating section. This is going to disclose all the information about expenses and revenue for any activities that aren't a part of the regular operations of the company. If your company sells investment securities or real estate in addition to your regular work, then you would list any profits you made from those sales in the non-operating section.

You may hear many different terms when it comes to the income statement. You may hear about income, earnings, and profits. These all mean the same thing so keep this in mind when you hear them. There are also two basic formats that you can use with the income statement, the single-step format or the multi-step format.

The Multi-Step Format
Some of the parts that are going to be shown in the multi-step format include:

- Net sales
- Cost of sales
- Gross income
- Selling, general, and administrative expenses
- Taxes
- Pretax income
- Other income and expenses
- Operating income
- Net income after taxes

The Single-Step Format
Some of the steps that come with the single-step format include:

- Net income
- Taxes
- Pretax income
- Other income and expenses
- Research and development expenses
- Marketing and administrative
- Materials and production
- Net sales

You can choose the method that works the best for your business and will include all the information about your own finances.

Statement of Owner's Equity

The next financial statement to look at is the Owner's Equity Statement. This is a financial document that can be used either on its own as a separate statement or it can be something included in the income statements or the balance sheet. It is sometimes also known as a Statement of Retained Earnings. This is the statement that will let you show the standing of your business earnings.

Often you are going to see this type of statement in a corporation that has a lot of shareholders and pays out dividends. But you can still find it useful with your small business in order to show your financial standings and your retained earnings. The main reason to use this statement is to release all this financial information to the public, giving the public the information they need to decide if they would like to invest in the business. It is also a good tool to analyze how healthy your business is.

The statement of owner's equity will represent the value of a business after it has met all of its obligations through a specific period of time. This statement is responsible for showing the movement of capital throughout that company and will reflect the amount that the owner or owners invested into the company along with any profits that the business has been able to generate that is then reinvested directly into the company. The reinvested income will be known as retained earnings on this sheet.

This statement is going to report the changes in the owner's equity over a period of time, and this time period is usually going to be for each year. As a small business, there is a chance that you won't need to use this statement because smaller businesses are more likely to report the retained earnings on the balance sheet instead.

If you do decide that your business needs to prepare the statement of owner's equity, you will want to prepare it after you are done with the income statement. This is because this particular statement will need to have the net income or the net loss for the period. But you can prepare this before the balance sheet because the owner's equity will need to be on the balance sheet as well.

This statement is a good one to use because it will help you to see the financial health of a business. It can also give you some insight into whether or not the business has sufficient cash flow to help fund its own operations without needing the aid of any outside investment.

Most of the time, you don't want to see a company reinvest their profits into the business because this can show that they are not doing a great job of handling their cash flow. But, if the business is growing really quickly, the owners may decide to invest some capital to help fund additional wages, accounts receivable, and inventory to help them keep up. This is acceptable because that money will easily be made back shortly once they catch up a bit.

The problem is if the business is not able to support itself financially without these capital infusions. If the business does this statement and it is not able to support itself without these infusions of capital, then the creditors are not likely to work with the business and it can be hard to get the loan that you need to run your business.

Cash Flow Statement

The cash flow statement is going to show you the flow of cash that comes into and out of your business. It is able to do this by splitting this information up into four parts. These parts include:

- Operating activities: This will convert the items that are found on your prepared income statement from the accrual basis of accounting to cash.
- Investing activities: This lists the purchases and the sales that occur from any of your long-term investments, your property, or your plant and equipment.
- Financing activities: This is the report that will show the issuance and the repurchase of company bonds and stocks. It will also include information about payments of the dividends.
- Supplemental information: This is the report will show any exchange of significant items. These are items that do not involve any cash and can report the number of income interests and taxes that the company pays out.

The statement of cash flows, also known as the cash flow statement, is a financial statement that most businesses need to use in order to summarize the amount of cash, as well as cash equivalents, that enter and leave the company.

This statement is important for measuring how well a company is able to manage the position it has with cash. What this means is how well the company is able to generate cash or profits in order to fund any operating expenses it has and any debt obligations it needs to pay out. The cash flow statement works along with the income statement and the balance sheet and it has been a mandatory part of financial reports for a company since 1987.

The cash flow statement is going to be very useful for a company. It is going to allow lenders and investors to have a better understanding of how a company's operations are going, where the money for a company comes from, and how that money is being spent. It is so important because it will ensure that lenders and investors have the right information to determine whether a particular company is financially secure or not.

Creditors will often use this information to help them determine the amount of cash that the company has readily available. The company needs to have this money to help them pay off debts and pay their operating expenses. If the company doesn't have enough cash based on their debts and operating costs, it may not look that great for the company and the creditor may not offer the loan to them.

The main components that come with the cash flow statement of the company include:

- Cash from all the operating activities
- Cash from investing activities of the company
- Cash from any financing activities that the business has
- Any noncash activities. These are sometimes included but will depend on the business.

It is important to know that the cash flow statement is going to hold different information, compared to the balance sheet and the income statement. This is because it is not going to include the amount of the future cash that comes in and goes out. This information will be recorded on credit. What this means is that the cash of the company is not the same thing as the net income, which is found on the balance sheet and income statement, which includes sales and the cash sales made on credit.

These sections can hold onto a lot of different information, and the parts that you fill in will depend on what your business does. Let's break down each of these sections to help see what information needs to go inside each one when you do your bookkeeping.

Operating Activities
- Other liabilities that are current
- Unearned revenues
- Income taxes payable
- Interest payable
- Payroll taxes payable
- Wages payable
- Accounts payable
- Notes payable
- Other current assets

- Prepaid insurance
- Supplies
- Inventory
- Accounts receivable

Investing Activities

- Vehicles
- Furniture and fixtures
- Equipment
- Buildings
- Land
- Any long-term investments

Financing Activities

- Treasury stock
- Retained earnings
- Paid-in capital from your treasury stock
- Paid-in capital in excess of par-preferred stock
- Preferred stock
- Deferred income taxes
- Bonds payable
- Notes payable (ones that are usually due after a year)

Supplemental Information

This is going to include anything else that shows the flow of cash into and out of the business that is not covered in the above categories.

Chapter 7:

Understanding How Taxes Work for Your Small Business

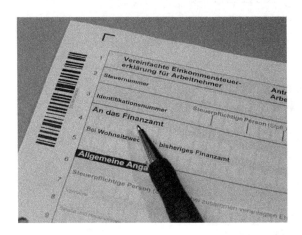

In addition to helping you keep track of the financial information for your business, doing well with your bookkeeping can help you get prepared when it is time for tax season. Many new business owners feel a bit overwhelmed when it is time to do their taxes. But if you have maintained your books through the year, then tax time is going to be easy.

There are a few things that you need to know before filing your federal income tax. As a small business, you may make the mistake of thinking the IRS is not concerned with your tax liability. However, the IRS does care quite a bit. This chapter will take a look at some of the things that you should watch out for when it comes to working on your taxes.

The Legal Entity You Choose Can Affect Your Tax Burden

Your small business may not have to shoulder the same tax burden that another one does. The legal entity that you go with can have a bit effect on the amount of tax liability that you have throughout the years.

There are different types of entities that your business can choose. You can be a sole proprietorship, an LLC or an S corporation to name a few. The S corporation is beneficial because it allowed you the advantage of being able to pay your taxes at the same level as a shareholder, but it does limit how many stocks you can use. The C corporation can help you deduct more expenses at tax time, but it includes double taxation and a lot more paperwork compared to others.

You should carefully look through your business and decide which of these entities is the best one for your needs. Each one has a benefit and some negatives, so you want to look through them all to make sure that you pick out the best one for your needs.

You Can Sometimes Deduct More Than You Think

As a small business, you are probably used to having to stretch out your budget as far as possible. You may not have the stockholders to rely on and you certainly don't have the large budget that some of the capital that the bigger companies should have. Despite this smaller business budget, you still need to pay for raw materials, rent for the building you use, the salaries of any employees you hire, the operational costs, and even utilities. The good news is that a small business owner is able to deduct many of these expenses and lower their tax burdens so they can stretch their business profits further.

According to information from the IRS, a business is able to deduct any expense that is deemed necessary and ordinary for that industry. These ordinary expenses are going to be any of those that are common for your specific trade. Necessary expenses are the ones that make your work easier but aren't necessarily used by every business.

There are a lot of expenses that can fall into this and that you are able to deduct when it is tax season. You can deduct the rent on your home office or business, computers, office equipment, supplies, and more. In addition, small businesses can deduct the costs that they pay when providing healthcare benefits to any employees. You should take the time to research all of the deductions that apply to you to help save money and lessen your tax bill.

It is important that you go through all the deductions and see if they pertain to you. This is one of the best ways to help you save money on the amount that you pay in taxes. You can then put this money back into your business and see it grow some more.

Remember Those Startup Expenses

One mistake that a new startup will make is thinking that the expenses they incur for starting a business can't be deducted. However, the IRS will allow small business owners to deduct quite a few of their startup expenses, even the ones that occur before they open their doors.

Although the expenses for starting up a business will differ depending on the industry, most businesses could deduce any investigational costs they incur when analyzing products and researching the market for their product. You can deduce costs for training employees, going to trade shows, locating suppliers, and even advertising to your potential employees.

One thing to note here is that you can only deduct the expenses that lead to the creation of a viable business entity. If you decide, after going through these expenses, not to form the business, then these costs become personal expenses, and it is possible that none of them will be deductible.

If you want to claim some of the expenses that you incurred while opening the business, you must keep good records ahead of time. This will make it easier to prove these expenses at tax time. If you keep them all organized through the year, it will also save you time having to search through everything later to find this information.

Make the Estimated Payments

As a new business owner, you probably know how important it is for you to pay your taxes accurately and on time. However, many self-employed persons are also responsible for making estimated tax payments each quarter through the year.

During your first year of operation, you are excused from making these estimated tax payments. However, you are still responsible for doing it in the second year and onwards. Business owners who file as sole proprietors or a partner in the S-corporation must all start making estimated tax payments any time they anticipate that they will owe $1,000 or more for that tax year.

You Must Pay the Self-Employment Tax

For those who are brand new to owning a business, you may not be sure what the self-employment tax is all about. This tax is comprised of the Medicare and Social Security taxes and it is owed by anyone who doesn't have employer withholding on them. Since you are self-employed and don't have your own employer any longer, you will be responsible for both your own portion and the portion that is usually paid by an employer to satisfy this tax.

To help ease their burden a little bit when it comes to tax time, you should try to deduct the employer-equivalent component of their self-employment tax. Doing this, and making sure that you claim all the right deductions will ensure that you are able to keep this tax as low as possible at the end of the year.

The Best Tax Deductions for Your Small Business

If you are new to running a small business, you may not know all of the expenses that you are able to deduct when it comes to tax time. Taking advantage of these deductions can make a big difference in how much your tax bill will be when tax season comes. Some of the best tax deductions that your small business should check out include:

- Vehicle expenses: Many small businesses use a vehicle to help them out. Operating that vehicle and the costs of it, for your business is deductible. But you must have proof and records that you used that vehicle for business.
- Wages and salaries: The payments that you make to employees, including their wages, salaries,

commissions, bonuses, and some taxable fringe benefits can be deducted from your expenses.

- Contract labor: Many small businesses are going to use independent contractors or freelancers to help them meet their labor needs. The cost of this contract labor can be deductible. If you are doing this, you need to issue a Form 1099-MISC to any contractor that receives $600 or more from you in that year. If you send them their payment through PayPal or credit card, then these companies will issue them a 1099-K, but it is still a good idea to send out the form for your own protection.

- Supplies: The cost of items that you purchased to run your business can be deductible. They need to be used specifically for the business, or you can't deduct them.

- Rent on your business property: If you rented out a space to conduct business in, then you can deduct this amount.

- Utilities: The electricity that you pay for the facility can be deductible. You can also deduct phone costs if it is used just for the business.

- Insurance: If you use insurance in your business, such as a business owner's policy or malpractice coverage, then you can deduct it at tax time. There are some rules when it comes to deducting health insurance though. A small business may qualify to claim a tax credit for a maximum of 50 percent of the premiums paid for employees, which is a better break than the deduction.

- Travel: If you or someone on your team travels to conduct the business, the cost of transportation and the lodging for that person is deductible. There are some exceptions to this. For example, commuting locally to work or to see clients is not going to count under this deduction.

- Advertising: Any of the ordinary costs of advertising your business can be deductible.

- Home office: A portion of your personal expenses for a home office is deductible during tax time if you use it for your business. If you conduct any business there, such as working on reports, meeting with clients and so on, then you can deduct some of these things for your taxes.
- Legal and professional fees: Anything that you pay for accounting or legal fees are fully deductible.
- Meals and entertainment: These costs can be deducted, but only up to 50 percent. So, if you take a client out to lunch to work on the business, half of it will be covered by taxes. The meal has to be used for business purposes or to further your business. You can't decide to take a break from work and count that unless you are actually conducting business during that lunch.
- Interest on any of your debts for the business: Any of the interest you pay on loans can be deductible. Starting in 2018, businesses that have the average annual gross receipts for the three prior years of over $25 million will be limited in the percentage of interest that you can deduct. And any interest on a personal loan that was used to help the business will be treated as well.
- Any employee benefit programs: The costs that you incur for any of the benefit programs you offer your employees, such as retirement plans, dependent care assistance, and education assistance, can be deductible. For someone who is self-employed, the contributions to their own retirement plans, the ones that are qualified, can be a personal deduction.
- Mortgage interest: A business that own realty is able to take the mortgage interest they play and fully deduct it. Unlike interest on a personal residence, there is not going to be a cap on the size of the loan where you can claim the interest.

Claiming all the business expenses that you have will do wonders to helping you limit the amount that you need to pay during tax time. You can work with your accountant to figure out which of these, and other deductions, you can use to help keep more money in your pocket during tax time.

How to Prepare W2's for Your Employees

If you have employees in your business, you will need to know how to prepare a W2. When you hire a new employee, you need to ask them to fill out a W4 for a regular employee, or a W9 for an independent contractor. You will need this information to help you prepare your W2s.

The W4 form needs to be on file with the business the whole time that the employee works with you. If there are changes that you need to make to this file, such as when an employee moves, then you need to have them fill out a new form. Before preparing the W2, make sure that all your employees take a look at their W4 to ensure that the information is up to date and accurate.

You will need to get all the information that the W2 requires. This will include the social security number of the employee (so it matches up when they do taxes), their name, address, how much they made and so on. Once you have all this information, you can then review and create your W2s.

Any employee who works for you at some point during the year will need to get a W2 from your business. It doesn't matter if they only worked for a few months or if they quit at the beginning of the year, or anything else. If they worked even one day for you during that fiscal year, then they need to get a W2.

There are several methods that you can use to get the W2 forms ready for printing. You can get them directly from the IRS, use a tax or accounting software, ask your CPA, or even purchase them from a local office supply store. When it comes to getting them from the IRS website, you are not able to directly download it from the site.

If you have the capabilities of doing this, an accounting software that has a payroll feature can help. You can just add this on and the work will be done with you. The accounting software can keep track of all the information for the year and then you just need to go through it and ensure the information is accurate before you print it off.

Next, you need to distribute the W2s so that your employees are able to use them on their own tax returns. You must get these to your employees by January 31st at the latest. You can either send out these out through the mail or you can have your employees pick them up. Some businesses are also choosing to have these documents available on a secured website to make it easier on everyone and to ensure that all the employees have a copy, won't lose it, and will get the information in time.

Once the employees all have their W2s, it is time to figure out how you are going to file them with the Social Security Administration. You need to file form W-3 complete with a copy A of each W2 for your employees. Two other methods you can use to file these forms include:

- File online at the business services online section of the Social Security website. You will need to go through some registration steps to file this electronically.
- Mail completed forms of W2 and W3 to the Social Security Administration

If you are in a state where the employee needs to pay their state taxes, then copy 1 of the W2 needs to be sent to the state taxing authority for each state that the employee worked in and paid taxes to.

Chapter 8:

The Best Bookkeeping Tips for Your Business

As a new entrepreneur, you have a lot of financial details that you have to keep track of to help the business run efficiently. Doing this well has a lot of advantages. It can help you to make sure that you are making profits and understand exactly where your money is going each month. It helps you to be prepared for tax season at the end of the year. And it can ensure that you are paying your employees properly and that your business is growing the way that you want.

Getting started with bookkeeping may seem a bit confusing when you first get started. There are a lot of different forms that you need to pay attention to, and this can be a bit scary for a lot of beginners who have never experienced these before. Let's take a look at some of the best bookkeeping tips that you can follow to help your business stay financially secure.

Plan for the Major Expenses

There are times when a big expense is going to come up. If you don't plan for these issues, you will either put yourself in trouble with money, miss out on some big opportunities, or have to go out with something. When you plan for these major expenses, and they are going to show up at some point, you will either have to miss out on a business opportunity that is important to you, or you may have to scramble for a loan from the bank if you have to pay. For example, if your computer system crashes and you need to pay for some IT to come in, it is much better to have this money on hand rather than scrambling to get a loan and get it fixed in time.

There are several things that you can do when this happens. First, put some big events, like a computer upgrade that is needed, on the calendar a year in advance. If you can, write this down every year for the next three to five years. You can also acknowledge on the calendar some of the seasonal ups and downs the business has and make sure that you are putting enough money aside to make it through these leaner months as well.

Often the costly things that you need to fix are going to show up in the slower months for your company. Do you really want to get caught in the trap of taking out money during the busy periods, just to find out that you are short on money for major repairs in some of the slower months?

Track All the Expenses

You want to keep accurate records of all the expenses and transactions that come up with your business. Tracking these not only give you a good idea on how the finances of the business are doing, but it can help you with tax season. If you don't keep good track of the expenses that you take on during the year, you might miss some tax write-offs or have to give up on a few because you just don't have the right information.

Having the right bookkeeping methods in place, and keeping all the receipts of your business along the way, can help you out here. You should either have everything added and uploaded to your online bookkeeping software or have another system of accounting that you can work with to help keep everything organized. This will go a long way in helping you see results.

This means that you should keep track of everything that you do with your business and every expense that you take for the business. This includes any events that take cash, any coffee dates, lunches, and business trips, should be kept track of. This habit is going to go a long way toward substantiating those items for your tax records in case you are audited. These records make sure that you are safe in case the IRS wants to look at your records and can make it easier to know what tax deductions you get in the first place.

Record the Deposits Correctly

The reason that this one is so important is that it makes it less likely that you are going to pay taxes on money that isn't income. You never want to pay more taxes than you need to, especially when it comes to paying it on money that isn't your income.

The best thing here is to take up a system that will keep all the financial activities of your business straight, whether it is a notebook that you use on a regular basis, the help of an Excel spreadsheet, or some software that can record all of your financial information.

As a business owner, you will need to make a wide variety of deposits into your bank account throughout a fiscal year, including deposits about revenue from any sales, cash infusions from the personal savings, or loans. The trouble here is that when the year ends, you (or a bookkeeping you decide to work with), might go through this information and then record some of the deposits as income when they aren't your income. And when this happens, you could end up paying taxes on more money than what you actually made that year.

Set Money Aside to Help You Pay for Your Taxes

If you are past your first year of business, or you are a sole proprietorship who owed the IRS $1,000 or more for a year, then you need to file quarterly tax returns. If you fail to do this, then the IRS could levy interest and penalties for not filing these on time.

The best thing to do here is to systematically put some of the money aside during the year that you can use to pay your taxes. Then, on the calendar, you will note the deadlines for the taxes, along with any preparation time if it is needed. This ensures that you are actually able to make the tax payments to the IRS on time when they are due.

One thing that can be especially problematic for your business is the payroll taxes. There are times when some entrepreneurs, who aren't taking care of their finances properly, will be crash-crunched and end up in a down cycle. They will dip into the employee withholdings, the money that was earmarked to be sent to the IRS.

If you start messing with these payroll taxes, you are going to end up with a two-fold problem. First, you haven't paid the taxes that are due for the employees, and you have taken money that the IRS sees as belonging to the employees. The IRS is not going to be very happy about this situation and you will end up in a lot of trouble. Set aside some money to help you pay your quarterly taxes.

Keep a Tab on the Invoices That You Have

You will quickly find in your business that any late bills or unpaid bills are going to cut into the cash flow that you have. When people are not paying the invoice that they owe to you, and you had to pay for employees to do the work and materials, this can really end up putting you behind. You had to pay for everything upfront and now you have to make due and keep getting things paid upfront for other customers, without having that money from the original customers.

You have to always keep track of the invoices that you have to make sure they are all paid on time. It is important to assign someone in your company to keep track of your billing. Then put a process in place so that you can make phone calls, send out a second invoice, and levying penalties, such as extra fees at a certain deadline.

When it comes to the invoices that you have, you want to make sure that you have a plan in place in case one of your customers doesn't pay their bill to you yet, since this can influence the cash flow so much. Come up with a plan of what you will need to do if the customer is 30, 60, or 90 days late on an invoice that you sent them.

Don't fall into the trap of thinking that once you sent out an invoice to a customer, that your billing is taken care of. Every late payment is basically an interest-free loan and it is going to seriously harm the cash flow of your business. You want to keep sending out invoices and have a good plan in place to ensure that you are getting the message out to your customer and that they will pay for the product or service.

Conclusion

Thank you for making it through to the end of *Bookkeeping*, let's hope it was informative and able to provide you with all of the tools you need to achieve your goals whatever they may be.

The next step is to put some of these practices to use. When you run your own small business, it is important for you to be able to handle all the invoicing, the cash flow, the debts, and everything else that relates to the finances of your business. Knowing how to handle all of these things can give you a good understanding of your finances and puts you in the best position to make good decisions for your business.

Whether you are starting your own business or have decided to take over the bookkeeping of your business to improve its financial state, make sure to follow the tips in this guidebook to help you get started.

Finally, if you found this book useful in any way, a review is always appreciated!

CPSIA information can be obtained
at www.ICGtesting.com
Printed in the USA
BVHW081024050919

557659BV00017B/1644/P